Remembrance Day

Why we remember

Cally Finsbury & Timothy Finsbury

Copyright © 2017 Cally Finsbury

All rights reserved.

ISBN: 9781973271895

DEDICATION

To Luke

CONTENTS

Acknowledgments   i

1 **Remembrance Day**   1

2 Did you know?   23

ACKNOWLEDGMENTS

To my wonderful helpers.

Remembrance Day

Timothy and his friend Dean were enjoying exploring the wonderful landscape.

Timothy looked at the beautiful poppies and smiled. Timothy loved flowers, he told his friend that the red flowers are a symbol and they are called poppies.

Dean had been curious why he'd seen so many people wearing poppies recently.

Timothy explained, "Mum had told me all about a special day called Armistice Day. This day is a day of peace which took place on the eleventh hour of the eleventh day of the eleventh month in 1918, which is why in the United Kingdom they hold two minutes of silence at 11am every November 11th. Mum will explain more to you about why poppies are worn on Remembrance Day."

"Will your mum be able to tell me the difference between Armistice Day and Remembrance Day?" asked Dean.

"I am sure she will. Although, she told me that Armistice Day is celebrated on November 11th each year, and this year it happens on a Saturday. Armistice Day marks the day the armistice was signed between the Allies and Germany that brought the end of World War One." replied Timothy.

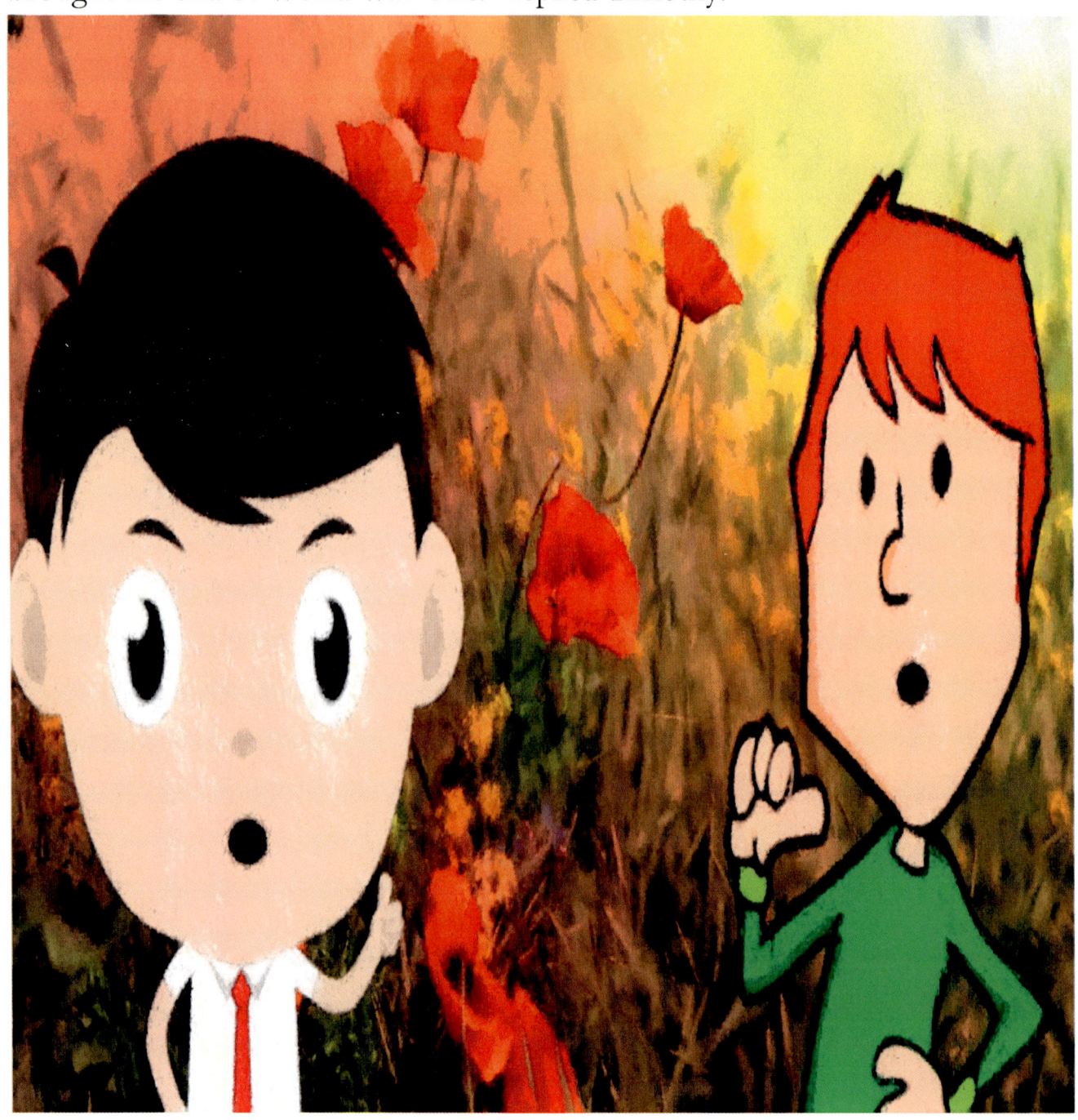

When Timothy got home, he asked Mum to explain more about Remembrance Day. Timothy's mum got out the prop box and explained, "A long time ago there was a war and when the war ended there had been many people who had lost their lives. The reason, poppies are worn is because they are the flowers which grew on the fields after the World War One ended."

"But why do they sell the poppies?" asked Dean.

"There are many reasons why they are sold. Some people think it is a good way to honour and remember those who have served during the war but one of the reasons is because The Royal British Legion is the charity which runs the poppy appeal each year and it gives the money to service women and men who are still alive and whose lives have been changed by war." replied Timothy's Mum.

Timothy's mum held up a poppy and showed it to Dean and Timothy. She explained, "There are lots of different designs and tributes with poppies, but they are all used to show respect."

"Timothy mentioned something about being silent to show respect, could you tell me more about that?" asked Dean.

"The armistice took place on the eleventh hour of the eleventh day of the eleventh month in 1918, which is why the United Kingdom they hold two minutes of silence at 11am every November 11th." replied Timothy's mum. "Does anything else happen on Remembrance Day?" asked Dean.

"As well as the two-minute silence to recognises the lost soldiers of World War One, World War Two and the 12,000 Britons who have died fighting in wars since 1945, a National Service of Remembrance is held at The Cenotaph in London's Whitehall on the Sunday." added Timothy's mum.

"Who watches or attends the service?" asked Dean.

Remembrance Day

"This service will be attended by members of the Royal Family, the Government, representatives from the armed forces and the public. This service will see a two-minute silence held at 11am before wreaths are laid and the Royal Marine buglers play The Last Post." added Timothy's mum.

"The Queen is getting older will she still laid a wreath this year?" asked Dean.

"Most of the soldiers that fought in the World War Two are getting really old so some are unable to walk or attend the service. The Queen has asked Prince Charles to lay a wreath for her on Remembrance Sunday." replied Timothy's mum.

"I would like to buy a poppy to help. I think I remember seeing them being sold in shops and super markets." said Dean.

"Yes, in the lead up to Remembrance Day, you'll see veterans all over the country selling poppies in various places and volunteers will also help to sell poppies." added Timothy's mum.

"I think I would like to find out more and to make a *'Did You Know Book'* about Remembrance Day." said Timothy.

"That sounds like a marvellous idea. You could also do a picture and I shall put it on the fridge." added Timothy's mum.

2 DID YOU KNOW?

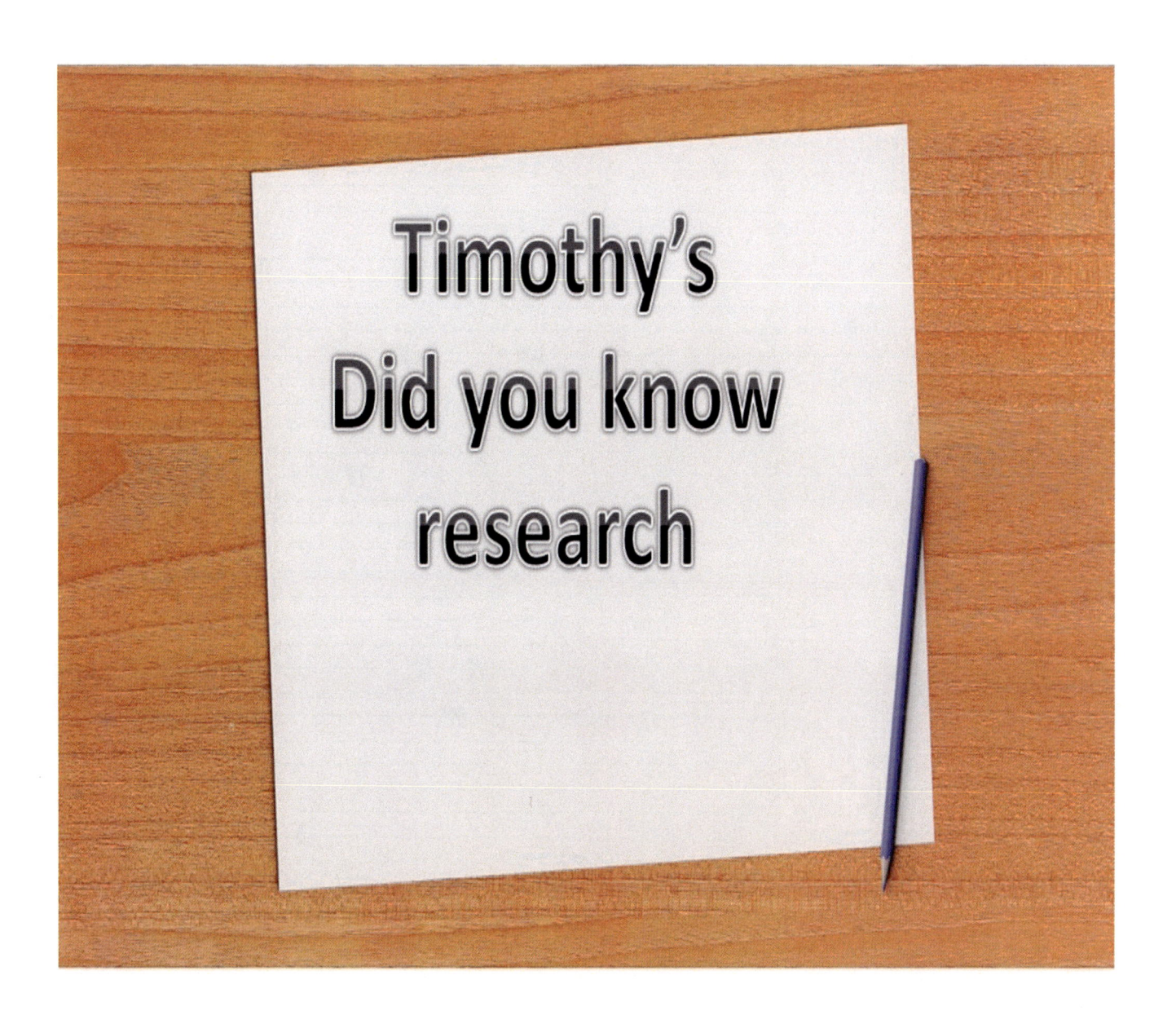

Timothy's Did you know research

Did you know?

Armistice Day is on 11 November and is also known as Remembrance Day.

Did you know?

Remembrance Day marks the day World War One ended, at 11am on the 11th day of the 11th month, in 1918.

Did you know?

That many people around the world hold a two-minute silence at 11am to remember the people who have died fighting in wars.

Did you know?

There is also a Remembrance Sunday every year, which falls on the second Sunday in November.
This year, it will take place on Sunday 12th November.

Did you know?

On Remembrance Sunday, there are numerous ceremonies at war memorials, cenotaphs and churches throughout the country, as well as around the world.

Did you know?

The Cenotaph was unveiled on 11th November 1920.

Did you know?

This is called The Cenotaph, Whitehall.

Whitehall, Westminster, London SW1A 2ET.

Did you know?

The Royal Family and important politicians meet at The Cenotaph in Whitehall, London, for a very special memorial service.

Did you know?

Remembrance Sunday is used to remember all the people who have died in any war. This includes World War Two, the Falklands War, the Gulf War, and battles in Afghanistan and Iraq.

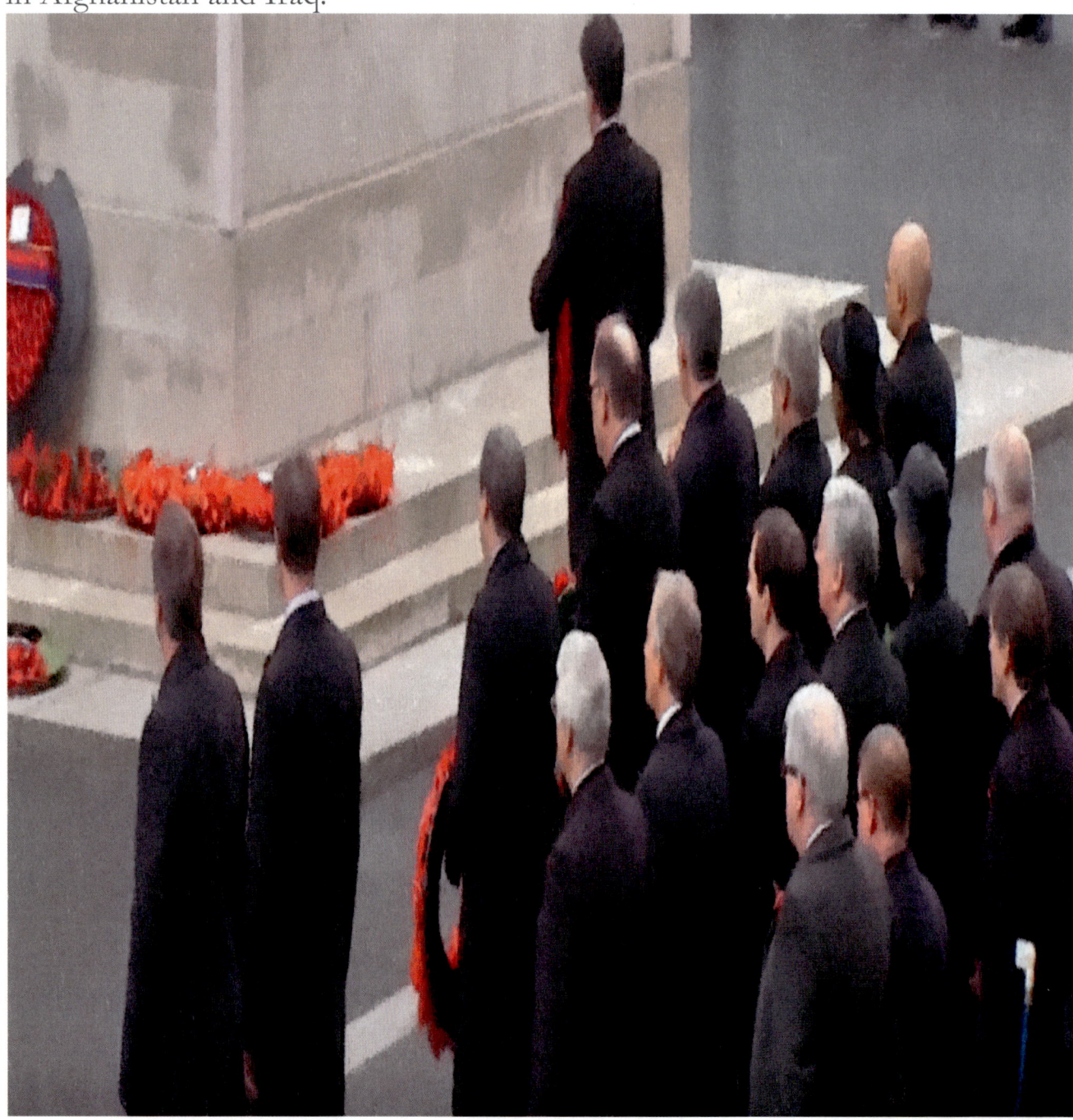

Did you know?

There is a famous poem called 'In Flanders Fields'. After the First World War, the poppy was adopted as a symbol of Remembrance.
Did you know?

A band performs at the service.

ABOUT THE AUTHOR

Cally Finsbury and Timothy Finsbury are a writing team.

This book is a work of fiction. Names, characters, places and incidents are either the product of the author's imagination or are used fictionally. Any resemblance to actual persons, living or dead, or to actual events or locales is entirely coincidental.

This e-book is licensed for your personal enjoyment only. This e-book may not be resold or given away to other people. If you like to share this book with another person, please purchase an additional copy for each person you share it with.

Copyright © 2017 Cally Finsbury

All rights reserved. This book or any portion thereof may not be reproduced or used in any manner whatsoever without the express written permission of the publisher except for the use of brief quotations in a book review.

somespecialpeople@gmail.com

Cally Finsbury

Made in the USA
Lexington, KY
31 August 2019